C000069950

POCKET BOOK OF

BALANCE

First published in Great Britain 2019 by Trigger

Trigger is a trading style of Shaw Callaghan Ltd & Shaw Callaghan 23 USA, INC.

The Foundation Centre

Navigation House, 48 Millgate, Newark

Nottinghamshire NG24 4TS UK

www.triggerpublishing.com

Copyright © Trigger Publishing 2019

British Library Cataloguing-in-Publication data

A CIP catalogue record for this book is available upon request from the British Library

ISBN: 978-1-78956-137-1

Trigger Publishing has asserted their right under the Copyright, Design and Patents Act 1988 to be identified as the author of this work

Cover design and typeset by Fusion Graphic Design Ltd.

Printed and bound in Dubai by Oriental Press

Paper from responsible sources

POCKET BOOK OF

BALANCE

TRIGGER™
The mental health & wellbeing publisher

www.triggerpublishing.com

the Shaw mind
FOUNDATION

Creating hope for children,
adults and families

INTRODUCTION

Modern life can be filled with so much: from the daily commute, a hectic schedule, cooking an evening meal; to those crucial turning points: quitting your job, moving house, finding love. Between the noise, it can be hard to find those all-important moments of quiet.

The Pocket Book of Balance offers a little guidance for when the scales of life are tipped, times become turbulent and a moment of stillness is needed. From the minds of some of the world's most well-known figures, learn to find your footing, take a breath and stand on stable ground once more.

Our lives are a mixture of different roles.
Most of us are doing the best we can
to find whatever the right balance is ...
For me, that balance is family,
work, and service

Hillary Rodham Clinton

Do not take life too seriously.
You will never get out of it alive

Elbert Hubbard

What I tell my kids is, 'I'm preparing you for college and for life. So, having independence, knowing how to set your own boundaries, figuring out how to make that balance.'

Michelle Obama

I do find that there's a fine balance
between preparation and seeing
what happens naturally

Timothee Chalamet

Like with anything in life, find the
balance between too much
work and being too lazy;
between spending too much
and being a scrooge ...

... between being gone all the time
and being in each other's way;
between talking each other's ears
off and dead silence

Christian Olsen

Live a life that is well balanced;
don't do things in excess

Daniel Smith

Balance isn't something you
achieve "someday"

Nick Vujicic

Balancing on a rope requires skill, steady feet, a steady mind and a sense of weight control. As you can see, the act of balancing consists of several things. Some of these things may be small ...

... but at the same time necessary to put the act together. A lot of people find it hard to balance work

Ginel Love

Wise men speak because they have something to say; fools because they have to say something

Plato

Balance is good, because one extreme
or the other leads to misery,
and I've spent a lot of my life at
one of those extremes

Trent Reznor

A good method of juggling different tasks is to always balance the short and long term tasks

Gretchen Pilar

When it comes to balance, you have
been sold a bill of goods.
It's time to give yourself a break,
embrace the life you have,
and make adjustments ...

... that will allow you to grow in the areas that are crucial to your most important commitments as well as your happiness

Dan Thurmon

You will never find time for anything.
If you want time, you must make it

Charles Buxton

Self-esteem is a matter of balance.
Too much can tip over into haughtiness,
arrogance, and the inability to admit
when we have gone wrong

Alan Schmidt

Our culture doesn't always promote balance.
Instead, we want everything instantly,
and we are willing to pay a premium later.
We're impatient

Jeff Kooz

Never get so busy making a living
that you forget to make a life

Dolly Parton

I don't like the word 'juggling' or 'work-life balance'. You prioritize

Joanna Coles

We are all tasked to balance
and optimize ourselves

Mae Jemison

There is no such thing as perfect,
and balance will look different
from person to person

Rachel Dresdale

Take some time to learn which
opinions you need to value and
which ones you simply need
to stop listening to ...

... Once you find the balance,
you are one step closer to finding that
confidence that you long for

Frankie Robinson

Having time for everything that's important to me makes me feel very balanced, relaxed, and optimistic

Steve Pavlina

Happiness is not a matter of intensity
but of balance and order and
rhythm and harmony

Thomas Merton

When we put balance to work in each area of our lives, we truly experience greater balance, greater reward

Jeff Kooz

You should learn to live a balanced life
while overcoming problems and accepting
each other's strength and weaknesses

Adam Green

When we refuse to balance the overwhelming demands of work, home, family, friends, and personal growth, stress will be the natural result

Mary Southerland

When you can, it's good to make healthy choices. But, I also believe in balance. It's not about being 100% this way or that way. It's about making healthy choices when you can

Miranda Kerr

Live a balanced life – learn some and
think some and draw and paint
and sing and dance and play and
work every day some

Robert Fulghum

For fast-acting relief, try slowing down

Lily Tomlin

I'm a believer in the parent first,
friend second philosophy, and trying
to find that balance

Jenna Fischer

The foundation stones for a
balanced success are honesty, character,
integrity, faith, love and loyalty

Zig Ziglar

While it is important to love others
unselfishly, it is crucial to find a balance.
When we compromise our needs
and martyr ourselves to the point of ...

... depleting ourselves and neglecting
our needs, we become out of balance

Jessica Minty

I've learned that you can't
have everything and do everything
at the same time

Oprah Winfrey

There's a balance to be sought
between being too much involved
and not involved enough

Mark Hodgson

If you focus on
negative and put out negative
every day, the scales of
life are off balance ...

... the only thing that can
return is the negative, you added no
positive to the scale to balance

B.W. Robertson

You can't do a good job if your job is all you do

Katie Thurmes

Perfection ruins the balance of life.
People wish for zero sadness,
zero death, zero illness,
and zero challenge ...

If all these 'bad' things are removed,
what are we going to live for?

Russell Davis

Wisdom is your perspective on life,
your sense of balance, your understanding
of how the various parts and principles
apply and relate to each other

Steven R. Covey

Balanced is not better time management,
but better boundary management.
Balanced means making choices and
enjoying those choices

Betsy Jacobson

In fact, everyone should take
time out once in a while to recharge
and revitalize their energy.
The key is to have a balanced life

Michael Lee

Many of us are trying to
balance work, home, and a family life.
We tend not to accept the early
symptoms of burnout and
carry on our daily lives.
In my opinion, living your life isn't
supposed to be that way ...

... If you ignore the red flags,
you'll become gravely ill
and your life could come
to a complete halt

Yasmeen Abdur-Rahman

It's really important to have balance,
spend some time in nature,
go to a few parties, enjoy my friends
and really chill out

Joakim Noah

I was a little, uh, incorrigible as a kid,
so the kitchen was a good place to give me
structure and balance. It taught me hard
work, but then I grew to love it

Aaron Sanchez

The creative people I admire seem to share many characteristics: a fierce restlessness. Healthy cynicism. A real world perspective. An ability to simplify. Restraint. Patience. A genuine balance of confidence and insecurity. And most important, humanity

David Droga

I like work/life separation,
not work/life balance.
What I mean by that is,
if I'm on, I want to be on
and maximally productive.
If I'm off, I don't want to
think about work ...

... When people strive for
work/life balance,
they end up blending them.
That's how you end up checking
email all day Saturday

Tim Ferriss

Serenity is the balance between good and bad, life and death, horrors and pleasures. Life is, as it were, defined by death ...

... If there wasn't death of things, then there wouldn't be any life to celebrate

Norman Davies

I think recharging is important, absolutely.
Every now and then, you need maybe a
couple of weeks to just chill out and let your
emotions balance themselves out a little bit

Malin Akerman

If you align expectations with reality,
you will never be disappointed

Terrell Owens

The body needs its rest, and sleep is extremely important in any health regimen. There should be three main things: ...

... eating, exercise and sleep.
All three together in the right balance
make for a truly healthy lifestyle

Rohit Shetty

There is no decision that we can
make that doesn't come with some sort
of balance or sacrifice

Simon Sinek

We all strive for balance, often moving
to extremes to find ourselves somewhere
in the middle where we can sustainably
exist in optimal inspiration. Working toward
balance takes a lot of ingredients ...

... We need courage, reflection, attention, action, and a push-and-pull relationship between effort and relaxation

Tara Stiles

When you have balance in your life,
work becomes an entirely different
experience. There is a passion
that moves you to ...

... a whole new level of fulfilment
and gratitude, and that's when
you can do your best ...
for yourself and for others

Cara Delevingne

I think if I manage to juggle a personal life
that I'm really happy with as well, as long
as I manage to maintain balance, that's kind
of the mark of success to me

Rose McIver

The best and safest thing is to keep
a balance in your life, acknowledge the
great powers around us and in us.
If you can do that, and live that way,
you are really a wise man

Euripedes

A well-developed sense of
humor is the pole that adds
balance to your steps as you
walk the tightrope of life

William Arthur Ward

To talk about balance, it's easier to
talk about what's out of balance.
And I think anytime that you have any
disease, and disease meaning
lack of ease, lack of flow ... dis–ease ...

... So any time there's disease,
you're out of balance,
whether it's jealousy, anger,
greed, anxiety, fear

Ricky Williams

Women need real moments of solitude
and self-reflection to balance out how
much of ourselves we give away

Barbara De Angelis

Beauty is only skin deep.
I think what's really important
is finding a balance of mind,
body and spirit

Jennifer Lopez

I learned a few years ago that
balance is the key to a happy and
successful life, and a huge part of achieving
that balance is to instil rituals into
your everyday life …

... a nutritious balanced diet,
daily exercise, time for yourself through
meditation, reading , journaling, yoga,
daily reflection, and setting goals

Gretchen Bieller

The people that I admire
have a wonderful balance
of self-belief and humility

Mahershala Ali

Overcome your barriers,
intend the best, and be patient.
You will enjoy more balance,
more growth, more income,
and more fun

Jack Canfield

There will always be another email
to get through; something to clean up,
file, and organize; more errands to do.
Which is why balance is so important.
Life is a marathon, not a sprint

Gretchen Butler

Everything in moderation,
and there's a perfect balance in
this life if we can find it

Ryan Robbins

Balance in general is difficult, but I refuse
to go through life and just have work
and not have good balance. I want to be
an example, not only to my own children but
also to artists and other entrepreneurs,
that you can be a workaholic and also be a
good husband and good father

Scooter Braun

The hardest thing to find in
life is balance – especially the more
success you have, the more you look
to the other side of the gate ...

... What do I need to stay grounded,
in touch, in love, connected, emotionally
balanced? Look within yourself

Celine Dion

Doubt can motivate you,
so don't be afraid of it.
Confidence and doubt are at two
ends of the scale, and you need both.
They balance each other out

Barbra Streisand

You want to strike that happy medium:
the balance of being able to find creative
satisfaction in your profession, be able to
afford a roof over your head, but still have
the freedom to live a relatively normal life

Chris Evans

Life is about balance,
and we all have to make the
effort in areas that we can to enable
us to make a difference

Orlando Bloom

My theme is, 'The spirit of friendship
is the balance of life.' Not money.
Not the World Series. It's friendship.
The relationships I have with people,
that's enough to keep me happy

Ernie Banks

Balance is key: I need to be successful
in my career to feel fulfilled,
be surrounded by people I care about
to share it with, and have my health to
be able to do the things I love to do!

Kiana Tom

Life is all about balance.
My work is very important to me,
but so are my relationships.
I make time for that aspect of
my life, and it makes me happy
having balance in my life

Samantha Barks

You can't start with imbalance and end
with peace, be that in your own body, in an
ecosystem or between a government and its
people. What we need to strive for is
not perfection, but balance

Ani DiFranco

A 'harmonized' life these days sounds like a tall order. Between housework, homework, workwork, and busywork, there are perpetually too many things to do, and not enough time to find that mythical balance ...

... Nothing is more frustrating than feeling like you're doing doing doing but getting nothing truly done that you really want

Jack Canfield

I surround myself with
positive, happy people.
And I always try to balance
things that I have to do
with things that I want to do

Nina Agdai

You have to find balance.
Whenever I start feeling stressed
or not feeling myself, it's about balance,
and it means I need to find it again

Bernard Sumner

I always try to balance the light with the heavy – a few tears of human spirit in with the sequins and the fringes

Bette Midler

One should see the world, and see himself as a scale with an equal balance of good and evil. When he does one good deed the scale is tipped to the good ...

... he and the world is saved. When he does one evil deed the scale is tipped to the bad – he and the world is destroyed

Maimonides

Getting in balance is not so much about adopting new strategies to change your behaviors, as it is about realigning yourself in all of your thoughts so as to create a balance between what you desire and how you conduct your life on a daily basis

Wayne Dyer

I feel like I needed a balance.
I don't want to forget about my personal life
and spending time with myself

Brandy Norwood

In this life, we are in a constant
search for inner peace. We long for it
in all aspects of our lives, both personally
and professionally. The truth is
that we cannot have inner peace
without balance ...

... It seems that having too much or too little of anything completely throws off our balance, therefore limiting our inner peace

Raheem DeVaughn

Because there is no cosmic point
to the life that each of us perceives
on this distant bit of dust
at the galaxy's edge ... there is all
the more reason for us to ...

... maintain in proper balance what we have here. Because there is nothing else. No thing. This is it. And quite enough, all in all

Gore Vidal

For me it's important to be in balance.
To not let fear get in the way of things,
to not worry so much about
protecting yourself all the time

John Frusciante

Everything is about balance.
You can't work, work, work, work
without any play

Janelle Monáe

Balance takes work. Lots of it.
There is no endpoint in balance, no goal,
no finalization. Balance requires practice,
patience, and – most importantly –
movement. We often get stuck in our ways
and form habits based on our fears and
driven by our insecurities

Tara Stiles

The trick to balance is to
not make sacrificing important
things become the norm

Simon Sinek

In life, there's a yin and a yang
and a balance. And when you don't
have balance, you have comedy

George Lopez

Focus on being balanced
– success is balance

Laila Ali

We benefit, intellectually and personally,
from the interplay between the
different selves, from the balance
between long-term contemplation
and short-term impulse ...

... We should be wary about tipping the scales too far. The community of selves shouldn't be a democracy, but it shouldn't be a dictatorship, either

Paul Bloom

Letting go helps us to live in a more peaceful state of mind and helps restore our balance. It allows others to be responsible for themselves and for us to take our hands off situations that do not belong to us. This frees us from unnecessary stress

Melody Beattie

Everyone's goals are the same
with very small differences. I mean, the goal
of a socialist and the goal of a libertarian
are exactly the same ...

... The goals are happiness and security and freedom, and you balance those ...

Penn Jillette

There's always a yin-yang in life.
With everybody. There's an evil in all of us.
It's just about how you balance out the evil
and the good and having faith in yourself
and how you carry yourself

Ski Mask the Slump God

It's about having an active lifestyle, staying healthy, and making the right decisions. Life is about balance

Apolo Ohno

I love what I do for a living–
it's the greatest job in the world–but you
have to survive an awful lot of attention that
you don't truly deserve and you have to live
up to your professional responsibilities,
and I'm always trying to balance that
with what is really important

Tom Hanks

When you feel sad, it's okay.
It's not the end of the world.
Everyone has those days when
you doubt yourself, and when
you feel like everything ...

... you do sucks, but then there's those days when you feel like Superman. It's just the balance of the world

Mac Miller

If somebody tells you that he or
she doesn't procrastinate, it's a lie.
In small doses, it can be even helpful.
If you don't take a pause from time
to time, you can burn out very quickly

Zoe McKay

I think health is the outcome
of finding a balance and some
satisfaction at the table

Alice Waters

Any time you start judging with
an overly critical eye rather than letting
things just be and following what you think
is right, it's complicated to find balance

Juliette Lewis

Balance is a feeling derived from
being whole and complete; it's a sense
of harmony. It is essential to maintaining
quality in life and work

Joshua Orange

You think you're getting sick this time every year because you over-schedule for the weeks leading up to Christmas and then you miraculously recover and vow to have a greater work-life balance

Kayley Loring

What I dream of is an
art of balance, of purity and
serenity devoid of troubling
or depressing subject
matter – a soothing ...

... calming influence of the mind,
rather like a good armchair
which provides relaxation
from physical fatigue

Henri Matisse

For a little guidance elsewhere ...

POCKET BOOK OF

RESILIENCE

For when life gets a little tough

POCKET BOOK OF
WISDOM

For when life gets a little tough

POCKET BOOK OF

COMPASSION

For when life gets a little tough

TRIGGER™

The mental health & wellbeing publisher

www.triggerpublishing.com

Trigger is a publishing house devoted to opening conversations about mental health. We tell the stories of people who have suffered from mental illnesses and recovered, so that others may learn from them.

the *Shaw* mind
FOUNDATION

Creating hope for children,
adults and families

www.shawmindfoundation.org

We aim to end the suffering and despair caused by mental health issues. Our goal is to make help and support available for every single person in society, from all walks of life. We will never stop offering hope. These are our promises.